Philip Parker

STICKLEBACKS

Illustrated by
Jackie Harland

PUFFIN BOOKS

Notes for parents and teachers

Each title in this series has been specially written and designed as a first natural history book for young readers. For less able readers there are introductory captions, while the more detailed text explains each illustration.

Contents

All the words that are in **bold** are explained in the glossary on page 31.

Three-spined stickleback fish.

These fish are called three-spined sticklebacks. Can you see why they are called three-spined? Look at their backs, they have three spikes on them. There are many different kinds of stickleback and they get their name from the number of **spines** they have.

Sticklebacks live in ponds and streams.

Three-spined sticklebacks live in ponds and streams but some can live in the sea. They are small fish, only about the size of your finger. They live together in very large groups. Each group is called a **shoal**.

The male changes colour and builds a nest.

Springtime is the **breeding season** for three-spined sticklebacks. The males leave the shoal to make their nests. The male's belly and throat turn red and his eyes turn blue. Each male builds his nest from water weeds, making sure that there is a tunnel large enough for females to swim through.

The male stickleback dances for the female.

A female three-spined stickleback comes to the male's nest. Look how her belly is swollen with eggs. The male sees that she is ready to lay her eggs, so he does not chase her away. He dances a zig-zag dance for her.

The female stickleback goes inside the nest.

After the dance, the female stickleback follows the male to the nest. He pokes his head into the tunnel to show her how to enter the nest. The nest is not very wide, so the female has to squeeze into the tunnel.

The female stickleback lays her eggs.

Now she is in the nest. Can you see the male? He is tickling her tail with his **snout**. This makes her lay about a hundred eggs. As soon as the last egg is laid, she leaves the nest and swims away. Often, more than one female will come to lay her eggs in the same nest.

The male stickleback swims through the nest.

Now the male swims through the nest. As he swims over the eggs he sprays them with a liquid from his body. This liquid is called **sperm**. The eggs have now been **fertilized**. Without the male's sperm, the stickleback eggs would not be able to grow.

The male stickleback looks after the eggs.

The male stickleback looks after the fertilized eggs. He uses his **fins** to fan water over them which keeps the eggs fresh and stops them being eaten by enemies. He will look after the eggs in this way for one to two weeks.

The young come out of their eggs.

After five days you can see the black eyes and tail of each new three-spined stickleback inside the eggs. When they are this young they are called **embryos**. When they are nine days old the young fish will wriggle until they **hatch** out of their jelly-like eggs.

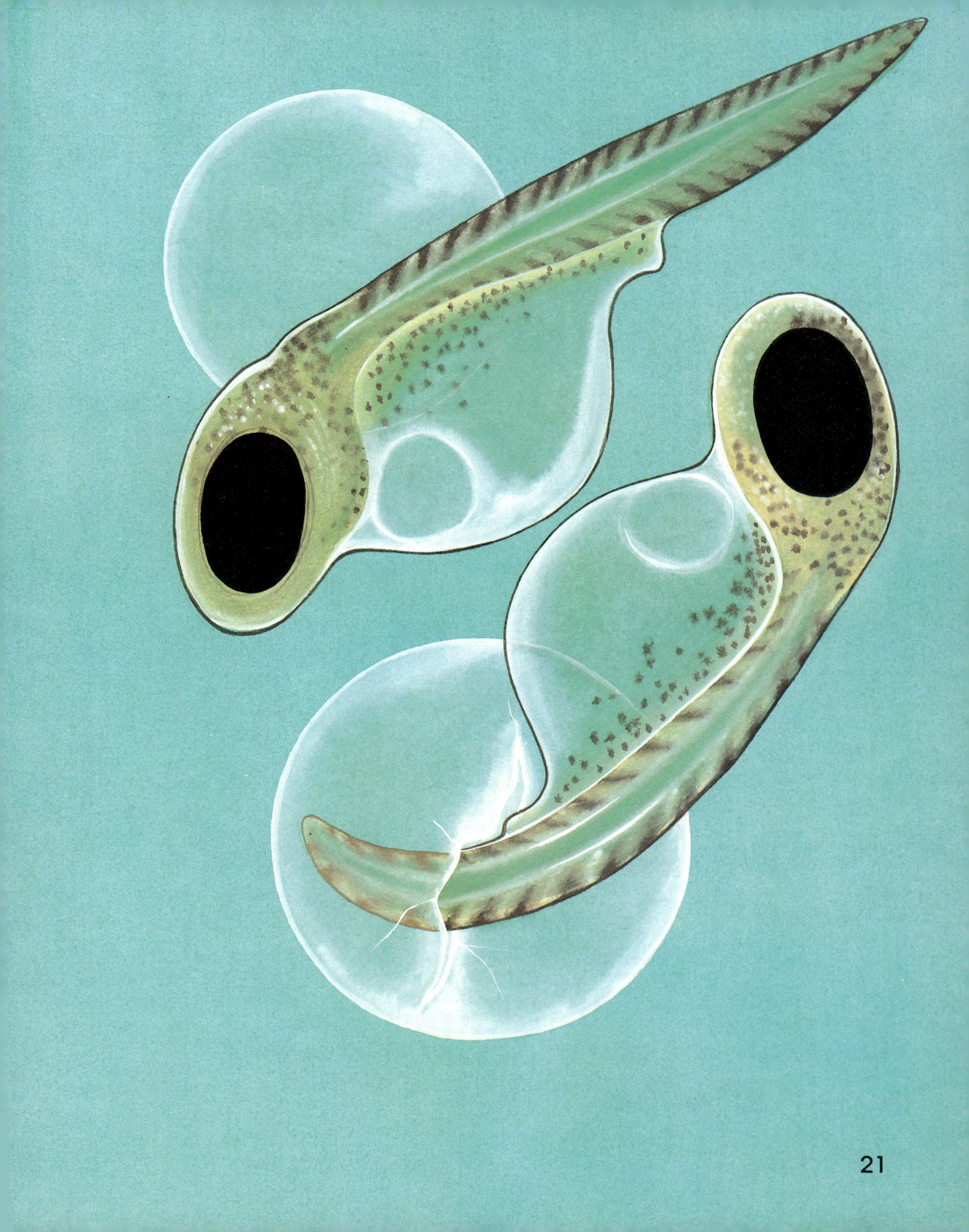

The young fish hide in the weeds.

For the first few days the young fish hide in the weeds to escape from enemies like larger fish and **water beetles**. The male stays to look after as many of them as he can.

The young sticklebacks are on their own.

It is four weeks since the fish hatched out of their eggs. The bright colours of their father have faded and he swims away. He leaves the young fish to look after themselves. Can you see the bright blue bird? He is called a **kingfisher**. He likes to eat young stickleback fish.

Fully-grown three-spined sticklebacks.

The young three-spined sticklebacks eat lots of different things like **water fleas, shrimps** and worms. When they are fully-grown they will be as long as your finger. Next spring each male will build his own nest. What do you think will happen then?

Keeping your own fish.

Sticklebacks cannot normally be bought in pet shops because they do not make good pets. If you would like to keep your own fish, goldfish are easy to look after. They must be kept in a fish tank or a fish bowl. Wash some small stones and put a layer in the bottom of the tank. Add some water weeds and wrap their ends around the stones.

Slowly fill the tank with water and leave it to settle for two days. Now you can put the fish carefully into the water. Feed your goldfish on a very small amount of dried fish food, bought from a pet shop. It is very important to keep the water clean. When the water starts to look dirty, fill a jar with clean water and leave it to settle for two hours. Carefully put the fish into the jar. Clean out the tank and rinse the stones well. Fill the tank with clean water. Leave the water to settle for two hours. Now you can put your fish back into their tank.

The life cycle of a stickleback.

How many stages of the life cycle of a stickleback can you remember?

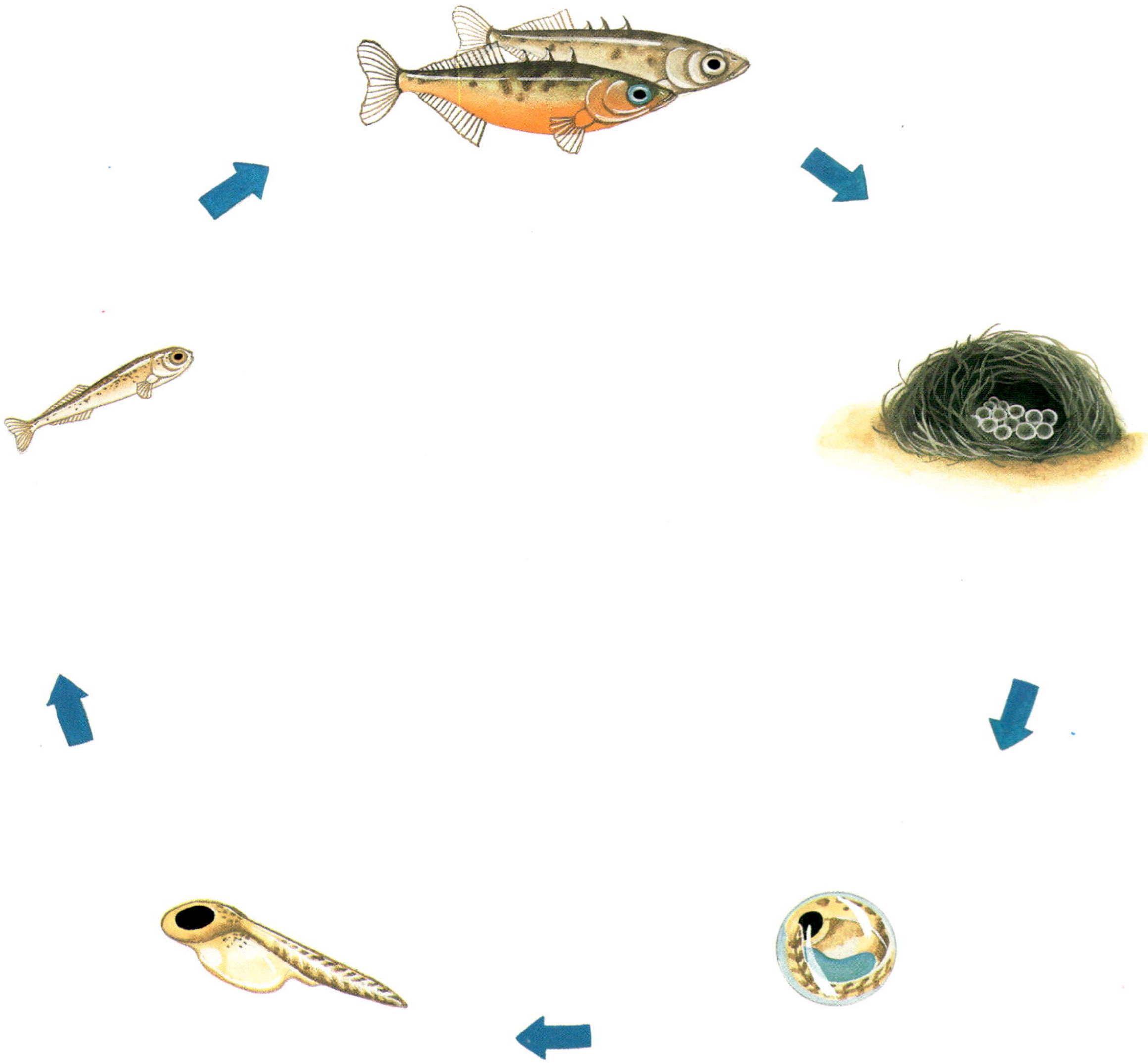

Glossary

Breeding season The special time of the year when different animals begin to make their young.

Embryos When the young are still inside the eggs we call them embryos.

Fertilized When the eggs have been mixed with **sperm** and they begin to grow, they have been fertilized.

Fins These grow on the body of a fish. They help fish to swim and steer through the water.

Hatch To break out of an egg.

Kingfisher A beautiful blue and orange bird that lives near water and feeds on fish.

Shoal A large group of fish that live together.

Shrimps Creatures with a pair of claws and a long tail that live in ponds, streams and the sea.

Snout The mouth, nose and jaws of a fish.

Sperm A liquid from the male stickleback which must mix with the eggs for them to grow.

Spines Hard, pointed spikes that grow out of the stickleback's back.

Water beetles Beetles that live in rivers and ponds.

Water fleas Tiny creatures that live in ponds and streams.

Finding out more

Here are some books to read to find out more about sticklebacks and other fish.

Discovering Freshwater Fish by B. Brewster (Wayland, 1987)
Discovering What Goldfish Do by S. Simon (Windmill, 1973)
Fishes by G. Vevers (The Bodley Head, 1974)
Freshwater Fishes by A. Wheeler (Kingfisher, 1983)
Lakes and Rivers by M. Cuisin (Ward Lock, 1979)

Index